PREPPING

FOR

FREE OR CHEAP

A Survival Guide To Get You Prepared For A
Disaster While Saving Money


By Dani Tippmann

First Edition

ISBN-13:
978-1535555159

ISBN-10:
1535555157

## DISCLAIMER:

### Introduction - Overview

America is in trouble and you can help. You've read all the articles and researched the financial cliff that is looming for our country. You know that there is a lot to be done and very little time to avoid an event that is very bad, if not tragic. You are also aware that there is always an emergency just around the corner, something that is going to happen, you just don't know when. Even if it isn't a national event that touches all Americans, there are emergency situations that happen throughout America every day. One will most likely touch your life in a personal way.

You need to be prepared and you want to do it with as little cash as possible. That's why having this book in your hands will start you in the right direction. We will walk through the steps to do things to prepare for a wide myriad of scenarios that could happen. The way that you are preparing for events can assume that you stay in place, or that you move to a remote area that you have pre-prepped for an evacuation event. In most situations, you will still need the basics that are presented in this book.

Every amateur who wants to become an expert, practices, and practices often! Do NOT set this book down to gather dust on your shelf! Take a look at it now. If you want to be prepared, then you need to learn and rehearse, NOW – while you still can. Once you are in an EOTWAWKI (End Of The World As We Know It) situation, there won't be time to read this information. You need the time to prepare and the first step is reading this book.

Just imagine, if you waited until tomorrow to read and put into practice what you learn, then you may never get the chance to prepare. Tomorrow may be the EOTWAWKI. If you start now, you are that much more prepared than you were before you started. Think of "preparing" as a savings account. If you  put a little away every day, after a year you have some savings accumulated. It may not be much, but it is more than what you started with. If, on the other hand, you never start an account, then after a year passes, you will have no more than you did the year before – Nothing! So, start your "prepper account" right now, by reading this book and putting into practice the knowledge you find here. Little by little, you will see your preparedness increase as time passes. After a year, you should step back and take a look at how much you have accomplished with just the knowledge in this book and your own initiative. You will be better prepared to meet future hardships.

Getting prepared does not have to be expensive. (That's what some of the prepper sites want you to think. They definitely want to get you prepared, but at what price?) In order to prepare, you should consider what something really costs. Why does it cost what it costs? Maybe it is made of expensive materials or components, or maybe it takes a special knowledge to produce it. Something that has value to you, that you would like to buy, may not have the same value to someone else.

There are costs involved in life. There are always costs involved in getting something that you want. We need to cut them and find a better and cheaper way to be ready. I know that this book is "Prepping For Cheap or Free," but maybe the book should be Prepping for little or no money. Paying for things takes many forms. Although you will learn how to "buy" things at a reduced price, you will also learn that other commodities can take the place of money. We don't have control of the actual cost of items, but we can make it so that we use less money to get an item.

If you can't change the price of something, how can you get it for a lesser monetary price? You are probably richer than you thought! You may not have cash in great heaps, just lying around, but you probably have other riches that can be substituted for cash. You will be able to think about spending and purchasing your needs and wants in a different light.

We should look at "purchases" that you make by what they are really worth. Your purchase of something not only gets you what you want, it gives the other person what they want as well. Remember to think about what the other person wants too. As long as you both are happy with the end result, and get what you both want, it was a "good deal."

Basically, there are always 4 commodities to deal with, all of which are interchangeable. The actual cost of something remains the same, but we get to choose how we pay for it. We can use any of the following, Money, Time, Effort or Energy, and Knowledge. Some combination of these four commodities will make up the actual cost of what we want to buy. After reading the following scenarios, you should understand the overall picture of the cost of an object.

Money

Time

Effort or Energy

Knowledge

Let's look at a few short, imaginary scenarios.

1. Suppose you just got off work and are on your way home. You are hungry and you want food. You can either:
   a. Stop by a friend's house to depend on their hospitality – This requires Time & Knowledge
   b. Go home and Start growing a garden – This requires Time, Effort & Knowledge
   c. Stop at a restaurant – requires Money

2. Suppose you want to know what the weather will be like in the morning.
   a. Buy a television and watch the weather report/prediction – Money and Time

b. Go to college, learn to predict the weather, buy the proper equipment and predict the weather – Money,

Time, Knowledge and Effort

c. Learn to watch the sky and nature's weather indications – Time, Effort and Knowledge

3. Suppose you want to get a new pair of shoes.
    a. Buy a pair - Money
    b. Kill a deer; Tan the hide; Cut out the pattern; Sew the shoes – Time, Effort & Knowledge

Sometimes the end-result is not what we really want to have and use. We may need a pair of work boots, but all that our knowledge will allow us to make is a pair of moccasins. Both are foot coverings, but one will just not allow us to do the same work that the other one will. We need to make certain that we can use what we bargain for. Don't go to the effort of getting something unless you really need or can use it.

At other times what we need we can make with our own two hands. Take the example of wanting a meal. If we plan ahead and start a garden in the

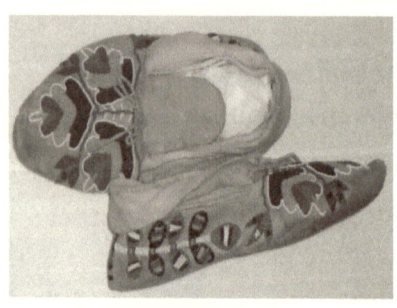

spring, or at least put some vegetable seeds in a container on the patio, then we can grow a salad for a future meal. This example would take a lot of time, effort and some knowledge too. If you did plant seeds, care for the plants and then harvest them for a meal, there would be costs associated with this method, although they may be minimal. Actual costs might include:

| Expense | New/Store Bought | Used/Bartered / Repurposed | Skill |
|---|---|---|---|
| | | | |
| Containers | $10.00 | Free (empty repurposed bottles) | Effort |
| Potting soil | $ 3.00 | Free(dirt from discarded potted flower) | Effort |
| Seeds | $ 1.00 | Free (Seed exchange) | Time |
| Water | $ 4.00 | Free (collect rain water to use on plant) | Effort |

The above explanation of the differences In ways to grow plants can account for whether or not there is money in your pocket and how much!

It does require some planning to be the person who has money in his pocket. I believe that because you are reading this book, you have

 already started planning and preparing for your future.

You should look at any purchase price of something as a combination of our four commodities, Money, Time, Energy/Effort & Knowledge. Preparing for a safe future does not have to cost a small fortune. You can prepare with minimum money out of your pocket, although it may cost you a little Time, Energy, Effort and Knowledge.

There are a few ways to make things happen that we will not be talking about in this book – the illegal ways to do things! This book will deal with legal and moral ways to make things happen. Stealing food or shoes, although an option, are not legal so we will not discuss that way of obtaining what you want. Do understand that other people may consider illegal options when they are in an emergency. You may need to prepare for their illegal actions too!

14

As you can see, there are quite a few legal and moral ways to make things happen. If you truly want to be independent and prepared for the next big disaster (and there always will be one happening somewhere), then take the time now to learn how to "Prep for Free or Cheap". It will not happen in a day. Start now so that you are that much more ahead of the person next to you. As soon as you are comfortable with your prepping, start helping someone else to become prepared. By helping them, you are helping yourself, because that one person that you helped to be prepared is one less person who will be fighting for the available resources during a disaster, resources that you or a loved one may need.

Money, Time, Knowledge and Effort offset one another. If you put in more effort, you do not need to put in as much money to get what you want. If you put in more money, you expect not to put in as much time or effort. It all comes down to working for what we want. If you put in the effort to get something for free you can save your money for things that you can't do or can't get for free.

By putting in more effort and some time into what you want, you can get what you need for free or a lot less money. This book will teach you how to do many of the primary preparations that you need in order to be prepared for the next disaster headed our way. Now you need to start working on putting these things in place when you can.

This book has goals that are in the order that makes the most sense for me. You can re-arrange them as you see fit and put them in the order that makes you the most prepared in the shortest amount of time for the least amount of money.

**The following is the list of subjects that need to be understood:**

**Primary Goal – Spiritual**
**Health – Air, Cleanliness**
**Water**
**Stealth**
**Reduce, Reuse, Repurpose**
**Food**

The above topics are in an appropriate order for me to accomplish being prepared in the order that I have found to make the most sense for me and where I live and how I live. Please feel free to change the order or to work on all of them at once, but maybe at a slower pace. After you have read the book, make the ideas your own and start preparing in the way that makes sense to you.

These topics: Spiritual, Health, Stealth, Reduction, Water, and Food are the subjects that need to be discussed and what needs to happen in order for you to initiate your preparedness. The rest of this book will deal with becoming prepared in the above order with as little money as possible.

## CHAPTER 1: PRIMARY GOAL

Be prepared spiritually. Someday there will be an end of the world – NOT an EOTWAWKI scenario, but a real end of the world. You and I may not be involved in that event. We might not be alive when it comes, but on the other hand we might be a part of it. It will be a cataclysmic event and everyone alive at the time will be involved, but you and I may not be. BUT for each of us there is an end of the world. An end to my personal world. An end to your personal world. The one thing that is certain in this life is death. (Not even taxes are certain.) Death is certain at some point in our life. No one gets out alive. So make peace with God. If you have a healthy inner, spiritual life, there is nothing to fear in death.

That could be the end of this book. Being prepared starts with you being ready interiorly, for eternity. Be happy with who you are right now, or go make things right!

If you have offences that need to be set right, relationships that need to be healed, or emotional or spiritual wounds that need to be healed, now is the time to take care of them. Think about it. Take time to pray and talk. Being in a good relationship with God is so important that, once you make the effort to get a good relationship with God, you should then take the time to keep it in good shape.

When you have a friend, you put time into keeping that friendship in good shape. Do the same thing with God. Talk to Him and keep your friendship in good shape.

Constant upkeep on a good relationship with God will make you stronger in all other parts of your life. God has loved us from the beginning of time. He wants to continue loving us. Make it easy for Him. Talk to Him.

I cannot overstress this first, primary point! You need to have your soul ready to meet your Maker. This is not something that you can put off until tomorrow. What if tomorrow is the end of your personal world? Take time – right now – to talk to God.

Throughout my day, I feel His presence. I know that God is a part of my life and I try to act in ways that reflect that knowledge.

IF you are ready for the end of your world, you can be at peace and ready to face whatever comes your way.

## CHAPTER 2: HEALTH

If you are to survive a crisis situation, you must be able to live. Life's physical necessities involve air, water and food and shelter. (Water, Food and Shelter will be covered under other sections, later in the book.) You can only live for a short while without air. We should be prepared to cope with situations where our air supply could be compromised.

You should be able to get through a crisis in a healthy way, provided that you have prepared.

**Air**

We breathe in and out every day between 17,000 and 30,000 times! Breathing is so automatic that we just don't think about it. Healthy air is something that we take for granted. In an emergency you may need to have breathing masks available.

A first step in preparations and an inexpensive way to be prepared for an emergency involving air and breath is to find the best facial masks that you can afford.

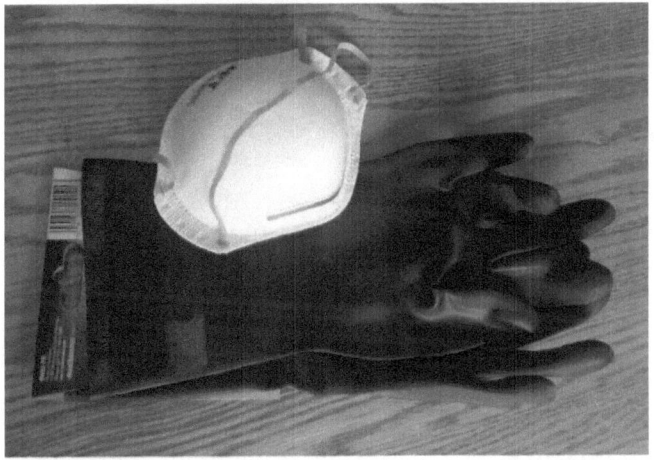

Some times that can mean simply covering your mouth with a cloth. If you start now, you may be able to find N-95 medical masks on sale or be able to find a rebate for them. These are good masks to have on hand. A particulate filter mask like the N-95 will help others around you if you have a cold or some other disease transmitted through coughs and sniffles, snot and breath.

For more intense needs, you may need to purchase an air tight mask or gas mask. You need to understand what you are buying. Research it. Some filter chemicals and others filter out germs. Understand what you want to buy. Spend some time comparing the products, then take the time to shop around. When you do have to spend your hard earned money, make sure it is worth the cost!

**Cleanliness**

In an emergency, you will be going through an increased amount of stress. The stress you are under can cause you to be more susceptible to germs. Cleanliness might not be a top priority when you are in an emergency, even though you may be more susceptible to certain preventable diseases. Once everyone in your party is out of immediate danger, you should begin to make cleanliness a part of the daily routine. Cleanliness can prevent diseases by removing the germs that cause them.

In our daily, non-emergency routines, we can easily wash our hands after using the restroom, and before preparing foods. In an emergency situation it becomes very important for us to make sure that everyone washes and keeps cleanliness in their daily tasks. It is so much easier to wash our hands

24

than to try to deal with a sick person during an emergency. If at all possible, keep healthy sanitary habits as a part of your normal routine and your emergency routine.

Keeping clean in an emergency doesn't have to cost a lot, but it could make all the  difference in how you survive and how long your group thrives.

There are pamphlets on health and cleanliness available through your local Board of Health and plenty of opportunities to learn about this subject on line for free as well. I won't dwell on the subject, except to say that it is important to learn and could keep your group healthier, during a crisis or in everyday life. It is worth the extra effort to be clean.

**Water**

Water mains burst, water can become contaminated, sewers can overflow, and rivers can become toxic (even when the EPA is involved).

There are many different ways for water to become very scarce in an emergency. We need water to stay alive.

Man y factors contribute to the amount of water that you will need every day. The ready.gov site suggests that you store at least 1 gallon of water per person per day for three days. That recommendation should be followed and other considerations to take into account would be a person's age, health, activity, diet, the climate and physical condition.  That should lead you to think about what the most likely event that would make you need water and prepare for that event with extenuating circumstances accounted for and you will have made the best preparations that you could. The www.ready.gov site recommends:

- "One gallon of water per person per day, for drinking and sanitation

26

- Children, nursing mothers and sick people may need more water
- A medical emergency might require additional water.
- If you live in a warm weather climate more water may be necessary. In very hot temperatures, water needs can double.
- Keep at least a three-day supply of water per person."

Please take time to visit the www.ready.gov website for many interesting tips on how to prepare for an emergency.

Even if you didn't have time to store water before a crisis, there is some water already stored in your home. Think about the clean-water pipes in your walls. Generally, they do have some water in them. This "hidden water" in your home is accessible to you in the event of an emergency. Also, think about your water heater. It may hold as much as 40 gallons of fresh, drinkable water. There is also the toilet tank (not the bowl) where fresh, clean water is stored for each flush refill. Tapping into these stores of water in your home can provide a small stash of drinkable water.

You must also think about conserving water as soon as possible during a crisis. Do not flush the toilet, if the water is not flowing to your home. Do not (obviously) do any extraneous cleaning. Make sure that you have paper towels, napkins, plastic utensils and paper plates around for meal time. Use sanitary wipes or paper towels with rubbing alcohol to keep germs at bay. Use very little water, and clean only as necessary. Save water for drinking. If you need to ration water, make sure everyone gets a full daily requirement of water. Use it for drinking. Keep hydrated! You may get more water tomorrow. Always drink the full daily requirement. Keep hydrated!

Before the crisis, on a day to day basis, make sure that you keep your laundry done and your dishes, pots and pans clean. This will make you prepared for short-term water crisis. If you let dirty dishes and dirty laundry pile up then it will be more work to make them clean or do without them in a water crisis. So keep on top of your daily chores. It makes emergencies just a little easier to cope with.

Make it a simple routine to:

- Keep yourself clean, including brushing teeth

- Keep your dirty laundry under control by doing laundry as often as necessary
- Keep the inside of your home manageable (this can be difficult with small children – let them help)
- Be organized (neat and tidy is easier to keep clean)
- Have a schedule of cleaning that gets done (this way nothing will be extremely dirty when it is needed)

If you can keep a simple routine of cleaning, it could make an emergency much easier to live through. It would also cut down on water usage during an emergency. That water may be needed for drinking and preserving life.

Because you are reading this book, let's assume that you have some time to prepare for a water shortage. Where should you store  water? Any clean leak proof container can work to store water. Some work better and some should be avoided.

Water can usually be stored easily in any container that held water before because it is designed to hold a liquid. I have used water bottles, plastic milk jugs and pop bottles. Of these three, the pop bottles seem to work best. If you store water in plastic milk jugs, change containers before one year passes because the jugs tend to leak at any seams. Do not re-use cardboard milk containers to hold water. If you use individual/personal water bottles they can be stored a little longer, and they can be hidden in smaller places as you conceal your stores of water in your home. (They fit behind bookcases and under couches easily.)

The 2-liter size pop bottles will last longer than either the personal water bottles or the plastic milk jugs. (Do not use milk jugs if at all possible. They often become brittle and leak.) Two-liter pop bottles are a little harder to hide, but still are small enough to blend in easily.

If you can get them, camping containers for water are excellent to hold your water. That is what they are meant for. Check second hand stores for camping gear especially water containers.

**Be sure to wash and sanitize any containers you will use for storing water!**

After thoroughly washing them in water and dishwashing soap, rinse them completely. Then to sanitize the containers, use a solution of 1 teaspoon of non-scented bleach and 1 quart of water. Make sure the sanitizing solution comes into contact with all the surfaces of the container. Then rinse with clean water.

Once the containers are cleaned and sanitized, you can fill them with water. If it is "city water" or commercially treated water then nothing else needs to be added to the water. If the water is from a well or is not treated, then you need to add 2 drops of non-scented liquid household chlorine bleach for each gallon of water being stored. It should have a slight chlorine smell.

How do you get containers for free?

Use the containers that are included with your juice or pop purchases. Better yet, ask friends and neighbors to save them for you. They make great containers for dry goods too. If you don't want to share information about preparing for emergencies then you can tell friends that you want the containers for holding and organizing things or for crafts. There are a lot of craft ideas that use sturdy 2-liter pop containers. I have seen people who are interested in crafts cut off the tops of pop bottles to use as organizers for small parts when they work on a project. (This is one way to use your

knowledge of people to get what you need for free. Glass canning jars can often be purchased at garage or tag sales or at estate auctions for a very small price. These

canning jars can be used over and over. All they need is a good washing and sanitizing. Make sure that they are not cracked or chipped before you purchase them. Some jars that look like they are able to fit a "regular" or "Wide Mouth" canning lid will not. Take a "ring" from both size jars with you to garage or tag sales to screw on the jar to check before you purchase jars. Just checking can save you a little money and frustration.

Many people use jars a few times and then decide that "canning" or "bottling" is not for them. If someone mentions that they won't be "putting up food" again, be sure to ask them about their unneeded jars. Always be on the lookout for other people's "cast offs." Just because someone else does not need or want something, does not mean that it is useless. You can give those jars a useful life and they will not take up any space in a landfill.

There are ways to have more water ready for emergencies too. Many local "Green" groups host workshops on water conservation and on water catchment systems. Look for free workshops that provide a take home completed project and information for your future use. A local museum hosted a rain barrel workshop and each participant took home a (food safe) rain barrel that stores 40 gallons of water for future use in gardens or flowerbeds.

Our local pop/soda bottling factory offers free barrels to anyone who will haul them away. I have used these as part of a rain catchment system because they once contained liquid ingredients for soda pop, therefore; these barrels are foodgrade containers.The water can then be used on our vegetable gardens. This saves on water procurement (either from the city or a well) and slows water down as it makes its way to either a sewer, ditch or river. It makes sense ecologically and financially to use a water catchment system, especially if you have a garden to water.

Once you have installed the catchment system, the water that you catch doesn't cost you anything. There is no fee from the water company for this water! It doesn't cost you anything to use. Gravity can provide the force to deliver the water through a hose to the plants you are watering. There is no bill from the electric company to power a pump to push the water to your plants! Keeping the water out of the septic or sewer system cuts down on long term maintenance costs associated with water. A water catchment and storage system really is a "long term freedom from bills" investment. Take the time to install it now. It will function during an emergency and still be free!

Being healthy means avoiding contagious diseases too. Keeping things clean and getting rid of filth and wastes is important.

Suppose you do not have any water coming into your home and are not able to flush the toilet because of the lack of water. This situation can be confronted with a large garbage bag lining the bowl of the toilet so that any excrement can be collected, contained and then disposed of out of doors.

To make your "Emergency Toilet" follow these simple directions:

1. Raise the lid and seat
2. Put heavy duty plastic bag into the bowl
3. Stretch the plastic bag opening over the rim of the toilet with enough plastic to ensure that it won't slip bag into the bowl
4. Lower the seat to help keep the plastic bag in place
5. Your plastic lined toilet is ready to use.

When the bag is full enough to be replaced, pull up the edges and securely close it. Then the bag and excrement can be buried or disposed of in a hygienic way. Try to bury the excrement as far away as possible from wells or other sources of water.

Using the plastic lined toilet for emergencies is a good idea, but you could also prepare now by getting a clean five-gallon bucket and keeping supplies for an emergency toilet in the bucket. I keep one in storage with plenty of heavy-duty plastic bags, an old toilet seat (for comfort), toilet paper, baby wipes, feminine pads & tampons, and lime to keep the smell to a minimum. If you wanted to spend a lot of money on this, you could go to a store that sells camping supplies and get a "back country toilet" for a small fortune that wouldn't be nearly as nice as the one you can create at home.

## CHAPTER 3: WATER

Water is the most important supply that you can store, that we will cover. Water is already in your home. There is water in the pipes in the walls of your home. You can access this water, even when the power is off, by opening the valve that is in the highest location in your home (maybe this is a sink in the upstairs bathroom). Next, go to the lowest point in the water system (maybe the washer hook up in the basement). Open the lowest valve and collect the water that will flow through the pipes to the lowest point. Depending on the size of your home, this can be quite a bit of water.

The water heater in your home can hold 40 or more gallons of useable water. Remember that it may be hot when you drain it for water usage in an emergency.

Another good tip is to clean the water heater regularly so that the particles that have settled out of your water are at a minimum when you need your water for an emergency situation. It is very simple to do in most cases. Most of the time all that is needed is to put a container under the spout at the bottom of the water heater and drain the settlement or "sludge" and water until the water is clear.

Other sources of water include rainwater. If your building has gutters, then place barrels at the downspout and catch this water for use. It will need to be purified before it is used for human consumption or for cleaning. We have already discussed in detail earlier in the book, how to get the catchment system for almost no money (and some energy and knowledge.)

Storing water for emergency usage is easy and free. It does take some time and a place to store it all.

Canning jars generally sit empty between use and harvest. These are wonderful to put water in for emergency usage. You have to store them anyway, why not keep them filled with water and working for you?

We have already covered rain barrels for water storage. Rain barrels, once installed, are free and easy to maintain. Definitely look for free food grade barrels. Many food producers, soft drink or soda pop bottlers and other food handlers dispose of food grade containers on a daily basis. Get to know the people who are in charge of disposing of these barrels and buckets! A call to a local factory can be a great start. Ask for food grade containers (You don't have to tell them why you are asking) for your free water storage system. Then go to a class on rain barrels or go to the library to learn the best way to install a water storage system for your circumstances.

Water catchment and storage systems can be expensive if someone else is putting it together and selling it to you. There are even "kits" that contain the parts to add to your barrel, to make your own system. This is a great example of our system of commodities. Depending on how much Time, Effort and Knowledge you put into your rain barrel water catchment system, you could put in very little money and have a high end water system in place before the inevitable crisis occurs.

You will also need a water purification system. This is

something that you should purchase. Look for sales, coupons and clearance items.

Get a map of your local area and check it out – NOW! Where are the bodies of water that could be harvested, if your water is cut off?

Most counties have on-line information sites on taxes and properties that are accessible by the general public for free. These maps can give you topographical information on your area as well.

Find the information that you will need in an emergency and print it out NOW. Plot out bodies of water and the easiest route to transport it to your home. Remember to think about how heavy water can be to

carry when you plot out the paths that you can take to carry your water. Check to see if there are paths that would allow a wheeled vehicle, motorized or not, to pass.

## CHAPTER 4: STEALTH

Just because you are preparing does not mean that everyone should know. When a discussion starts with you talking about what you have "put aside" for a very rainy day, it could end with raised eyebrows and comments about a "crazy relative". Once you start prepping, you may be excited about your newfound sense of accomplishment and the peace of mind that you have. But, it is not something that should be shared with everyone. Knowing how good you feel, it may seem like you should be sharing how to prep with everyone, but they may not be ready to understand it. Here are a few conversation starters that you might want to consider.

If someone asks about prepping you can try to make them understand that we all only have so much money. Each of us has (or at least many experts suggest that we should) divide it into savings for different things, including an emergency fund. Let's pretend that both you and your friend's

emergency fund is $100.00. He puts his in the bank and is lucky to make 1% interest on it. You have taken your $100.00 and invested in emergency gear and preparations. Your emergency fund has purchased preparations at today's prices, so any

purchase of gear that your friend would make could only buy less at tomorrow's higher prices, especially in the event of an emergency. And that assumes that there will be supplies to purchase during an emergency.

I like to start "prepping conversations" by letting the other person know that I believe that there will be an end to me and I have a need to be prepared for that. I think that it is very important to start our preparation for meeting God as soon as we believe in Him. After that preparing for things that happen on this earth are easy. If people are open to prepping for an afterlife they are usually open to prepping for life on earth too.

If someone notices your water and food stores and asks about them, you can always tell them how you spotted a great bargain and decided to act on it and have it stored properly so that you do not have to pay a higher price for quite a while in the future. When you are honest about how you feel about prepping, most people will listen and learn.

However, some people will not ever understand why you prepare for the possibilities that exist today. I would be very careful about who I share the full extent of my prepping with. Of course, my spouse knows all of the provisions that we have and knows how to use them. This only makes sense because my spouse would have to take over my role if something were to happen to me in an emergency. Even my children, who are too young, are not told about all the preparations that we have made in our home. Telling older children is necessary if they are mature enough to understand that the stores you have put away are there for your health and protection during an emergency.

Remember that when more than one person knows a secret, it is rarely a secret. You may want to think very carefully, about whom you share your preparati ons with.

If they do not understand, and make their own preparations, they may come to you for help in a real emergency. Then you have to decide if you want to share with him, meaning your family will have less. Another thing to think about is if your friend talks to others about your preparations, those people may try to TAKE your food and water and other stored items. Be thoughtful about who you talk to about your preparations.

"Hiding in plain sight" is a common way to make your preparations disappear. Many people will hide their preparations in very open places. Some good ideas that I have seen use common objects for storage, but they are not exactly what they seem to be. One example a friend uses is  his old, non-working freezer. He has drilled holes in it for safety (if a child would play in it, they could still breathe). It looks like a non-working piece of junk freezer, but is really filled with his prepping needs.

Another friend uses an old van that is parked in her back yard to double as a spare room for her preparations. Other friends use the space between their couch and the wall for storage. It makes a small area into a usable hidden space. Other friends bury things in their back yard for safety and it blends in very well.

Bookcases always seem to have extra space behind the books where you can stash a few things by placing the books on the front edge of the shelf. There are many other possibilities that will come to mind when you look around your home.

## CHAPTER 5: EASY

That title may be deceiving. It will not be easy to prep, but it can become second nature to constantly be in "prep mode." If you always keep a watch as to how you can be preparing for the future and you act on those thoughts, then you will become more prepared every day.

My thoughts are focused on my surroundings in the here and now, but I am always asking myself, "How can I be more prepared for whatever the future brings? " When I see an opportunity for preparation I try to take advantage of it quickly.

Hard work or Time is usually the next step after

identifying a possible opportunity to prepare for free. (Remember the Money, Work, Time and Knowledge composite.) Possibly some huge, empty, food grade containers caught your eye. Now you have to make the time to speak with the owner of the disposable containers and then you have to find a way to haul them home and prepare them for clean water storage. This is just one scenario, but you understand that hard work and time will be your investment in the future, instead of money.

Maybe in your "prep mode" you spotted some apples lying on the ground, under a neighbor's tree. Now all you have to do is ask the neighbor if they would like you to gather up and dispose of those apples for them. They can mow under the tree easier and you get the free fruit! Once the fruit is home, you will have to can, dry or freeze it for

future use.
Canning can
be your hobby
and it can be
very relaxing.
Knowing that
you are going
to have plenty
of food for the
future and
knowing that
you have
canning
Knowledge
and skills to

last a lifetime can be its own reward.

It's not always easy, but you can be prepared for what comes.

So be ready to ask neighbors (or the owner of any lawns with fruit lying under trees) for fallen fruit. They may want to have the fruit removed for free and you can get the free fruit. Stay open to other opportunities. Maybe they want some of the preserved fruit and you can barter your time and effort for their fruit. Maybe they will even pay for all the other necessities that go into preserving fruit, like sugar and spices or lids and you can put in the effort to preserve it. Do not be afraid to ask!

Next year, after you have already asked for permissio n this year, it will be easier to

obtain permission. You may even start a friendship because you both got what you wanted out of the situation.

Some people start a garden with excitement in the spring, but lose interest as the summer progresses. Talk with them about doing the gardening for a portion of the vegetables. You will make the garden look better to them and you can fill your larder with canned or frozen vegetables for the winter.

In some of the surrounding towns in my area of the U.S. "Appliance Days" or "Extra Days" or "Clean Out the Garage Days" are an added bonus for homeowners because they are given extra days or are allowed extra "trash" on their pick-up day. These days also become an added bonus for me! You can find many very usable, although not new, items. Some towns have a policy of no trash picking, so you'll have to remember to ask before you pick.

I like to ask the homeowners for permission before I take things home for their second life. Sometimes people just don't have the room to store what I've been looking for. Always check to make sure that the item you are considering is worth the effort. Some items can't be fixed and should be thrown out, others still have a lot of use in them.

Exchanging something that you see value in, for something that someone else does not see value in, is a great way to make a deal and have both parties be happy with the end result.

## CHAPTER 6: EDUCATION

Education is a big part of becoming prepared. Education can be very expensive, but it doesn't have to be. You probably have friends and acquaintances who have skills that are necessary for survival. Talk to people and really listen to what they know.

READ, READ, READ! Use your local library. It is free, entertaining and educational all at once.

Check out local and on-line colleges and universities. They offer free non-credit classes and they offer for-credit classes for free. Just check on line at the university or college website. Sometimes it's worth going to the college and checking with an advisor about free classes, especially if you want to get credit for the courses that you take.

College and university classes can be audited. This is free, but they do not offer any credit for this. You may have to ask permission to do it too. Auditing a class often means just listening to the professor and other students with very little interaction. The assignments will not be mandatory for most classes that are audited, but it would be best to complete the homework. Take the course seriously and learn as much as you can. You can gain an immense amount of education this way.

 Joining a re-enactor group to learn skills is a wonderful, hands-on way to learn very basic skills. You will be able to learn as you teach others too. Re-enactor groups that focus on early American history are fairly common across the nation. If you join as a family you will be teaching your children about patriotism and history as well as practical skills. Skills that are practiced by some re-enactor groups include shooting, fire making, camp

etiquette and cleanliness, and wild game preparation. This hobby can be very educational.

Other local organizations offer free or cheap classes including your local library. Your taxes already support your library so use it. In addition to classes, libraries offer classes on video.

When local organizations host open houses attend and see what they offer. Call to check if they have any free groups that meet with an intent to educate others. Some of the following organizations should be on your list:

YMCA/YWCA

Churches

Historical Societies

Herbal /Flower/ Gardener Societies

USDA/CRP

4-H groups

Agricultural Extension Offices

Some of these organizations teach skills such as canning foods, food preparation, computer usage, gardening, or raising animals. So make the most of your time and pick up a hobby in which you will learn a skill as well as enjoy yourself.

In every situation, be aware of your surroundings. You will become more educated because of your vigilance and awareness of what is happening around you.

Be willing to ask questions until you understand! It may be not be easy, but you can prepare with little or no money. Start by taking time to think and learn.

If you are proficient in some activity or craft, offer to teach it to someone else. I was a Cub Scout leader and a Boy Scout leader for a few years. I offered my time freely to the organization and helped to mold young minds into thinking adults. I also learned quite a bit through the field trips that I chaperoned, a free education opportunity! Once we toured a maple syrup operation, which gave me a few pointers for my own maple syrup operation. Another time our group made solar ovens. Another time I was a part of a group who planned and implemented a native plants garden for a local herbarium. There are always great opportunities to learn as you donate your time to organizations.

## CHAPTER 7: REDUCE

Remember and use the old adage, "Reduce, Reuse, Recycle!" This thought can be applied to prepping in a very successful manor. It applies to almost everything!

Reduce:

Think about your priorities. If you can live without it, maybe you do not really need it. Sometimes this can be difficult for

the rest of the family to co-operate with and fully understand. It is important to talk with your family members and make sure that they are on board with, not only prepping in general, but prepping as a priority that may interfere with their own personal wants. Asking them to be in charge of a theoretical disaster scenario and just talking through it may give them the thought processing time to see how important preparing is. This in turn will make them more understanding of the need to defer wants for needs when purchases are made.

When you get new products make sure to think about how it can be used for multiple purposes. Even something as simple as a bar of soap can be used in several ways.

Cleaning, of course, is one way. Another way would be to make a squeaky or stuck drawer pull out easier and quieter. (Note: Just rub the bar of soap on the "glides" in the drawer. This will reduce the friction and make the drawer pull out easier.) and use the empty soap bar box to scent your clothing drawer.

Another example would be how to use a food grinder. If it is a heavy-duty grinder then you can grind baby food, hamburger, wheat and/or other grains. Keeping things simple and useful is best.

Reducing also means that when you purchase something you try to make use of all of it. Another way to say that is, do not let anything go to waste. If there is packaging material with something that  you purchase, can it be used as it is or can it be repurposed to substitute for another item, so that you don't have to buy something else? An example would be if you bought oranges at the grocery. Of course you can eat the juicy orange, and you use the grated orange peel to flavor a food, but you can also use the net bag that the oranges come in. The net bag can be used to harvest nuts or fruits, to keep your catch in, during a fishing trip, to hold homegrown onions in, or tie the net bag into knots and use it as a "scrubby" when cleaning pots and pans; etc. This is just one example of using what we have to its utmost value.

Reuse:

Reusing things was very popular with generations past. It is only lately that disposable has come to equate with convenience. Think back to how people in your grandparent's generation used things over and over, time and again. Most of them did not expect to take the time to go to town and buy unnecessary and expensive things unless absolutely necessary.

A good, common example of this is a dinner napkin. Today, in our society, we buy paper napkins and we use them once and dispose of them after one use. If we make use of cloth table napkins we can use them many times over their lifetime. In my house, we have cloth napkins, and wash them once per week (unless the individual who uses it sees a need to wash it sooner.) This practice gives even longer life to table napkins and

keeps the laundry to a minimum as well as reducing the wear and tear on the washer and dryer and the napkins.

Think of things around your home that are "disposable" that you can replace with "re-useable" and thereby save money (and the environment as well).

Things on your list might include:

Cloth bags for presents instead of expensive and wasteful wrapping paper.

Video Games (Don't get the latest – borrow it from the library)

Empty Tin Cans (from food you ate) can replace those disposable plastic seed starters, or they make great bird house roofs or even can make shingles for your chicken coop (when flattened).

Wash your used "disposable" plastic bags and use them again.

Plates, bowls and cups – ceramic/glass is easy to reuse – even at the office or during a commute.

Paper Towels – They have their time, but not every day. Cloth is clean and easy.

It is important to note that if you do not have to replace something that it does not cost you anything. Be careful with the equipment that you already possess so that you do not have to spend time, money, knowledge or effort to replace it with new equipment. Be careful when you use it. Put it away properly. Clean it when it needs it. Really care for it. Maintenance is important.

Teach your children to treat equipment with care so that it does not have to be replaced. Teach them to respect all the work, time, effort or money that went into obtaining your equipment. Maybe they won't have to learn it the hard way when they are adults.

If you do need to replace equipment, be sure to think about how best to "dispose" of your old equipment. If there is any good left in it, get it! That can include selling the old equipment, or scrapping for metal content or keeping it for replacement parts for your new equipment. You can also give it to someone else who can still get some good out of it. When you do that you make that person better prepared and they are more likely to think of you if you need something in the future.

## CHAPTER 8: RECYCLE

Recycling should always be a possibility, but only after thinking about other re-purposing possibilities. It's always cheaper to have and re-use than it is to re-buy!

Most scrap yards are easy to access and it is a great way to clean up and make a few extra dollars. Before you go to the scrap metal recycler sort your metals. The easiest way to do this is to have a magnet handy and touch it to each piece as you load it for the trip to the recycler's (or better yet sort it as you are storing it). There are ferrous (iron containing metals) and non-ferrous metals (non-iron containing metals). Use the magnet to see if your metals are ferrous or non-ferrous in nature. If the magnet sticks to a metal, the metal contains iron and is a ferrous metal, such as steel or iron.

Some non-ferrous metals include copper aluminum, brass, and some wires. Non-ferrous metals currently are garnering a higher price than ferrous metals. It is easy to be aware of scrap metal prices. Most re-cyclers post their price on their website and on street signs near their business or you can call and ask. I try to estimate the weight of my scrap metal so that it will be at least the "Bonus Minimum Price," that many re-cyclers pay. This can add a few more cents per pound to the scrap metal price and it is worth waiting until your pick-up truck is a little fuller for the higher price. This also gives me fewer trips to the recycler and saves me gas and wear and tear on the vehicle in the long run.

## CHAPTER 9: SPARE TIME

Your spare time will become your moneymaker and your money saver. If you are serious about the future and being prepared for it, then you need to make time in your schedule. Commit to watching very few television shows (unless they teach or help you to prepare!). You will need to stay in touch with weather and other important news about your world though. I believe that listening to the radio for a few hours as "background" for my regular life's work helps me to stay in touch and more relaxed because of the knowledge I receive. You need to have some relaxation in your life and if television viewing is your way to unwind, then by all means, do it. Just remember that, "everything in moderation" is a good way to live (including how we spend our relaxation time.)

We do watch television in our home as entertainment, but we only get the stations that were known as the "Farmer 5." They are the free television channels that depend on advertising to make a living and do not depend on my money to support them.

As you go about your daily routine think of other ways to shorten your work load or take time from your "down time". Then add that time to your time to prepare for the future.

You might consider asking for a raise or getting a second job to add a little to your income. It may be worth it to just have the extra income during the time that you "found" in your schedule. But please examine and judge whether it is worth the extra effort.

Remember the old adage, "A penny saved is a penny earned?" Well that is more than true. If you can save money, instead of actually going out and getting a second job or a raise, then you have saved yourself paying taxes on the new income and, in essence, kept more of your money for yourself. Think of ways to save the money that you already have paid taxes on, then you are actually saving the amount that you would have paid in taxes plus what you did not spend. Keep being aware of ways to cut your costs and not put out any cash that is not absolutely necessary.

Instead of taking on more employment, it may be a better investment of your time to be at home getting free things for your preparations. This is something that you really need to take time and decide for your individual circumstances.

Another great way to create more cash and use your spare time is to learn a skill that you can turn into more income or save you money that you would have had to pay someone else for their skill.

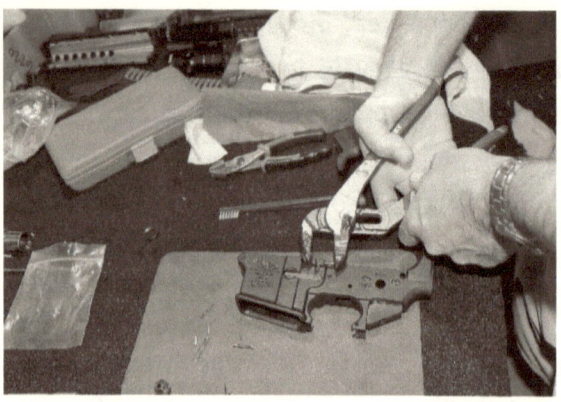

Another easy way to save money is to pay off any loans. Not having to pay interest on credit cards and car loans will save you money. Make do with what you have and do not spend money on the "next big thing" or the latest thing that "everyone else" has. Be the person who is happy with their life because they know they are prepared. You do not have to keep up with the Joneses to be happy. Being happy, for me, is within, it's not from things and comparing myself to others.

## CHAPTER 10: FOOD

There are several easy and cheap ways to fill your pantry with food. We will discuss couponing, gardens, and overflow in this section.

Couponing is easy. Coupons are like money. Coupons are everywhere. They are on the packages that food comes in, i.e. cans, bottles, boxes and tubs. They are available in stores at the purchase point of foods. These are easy to add to the coupons that you use because they are at the point of sale of the food. They are displayed to attract your attention in a convenient location.

Another way to get coupons is on Saturdays at major retailers through "product tastings" or "free samples." Coupons are in flyers; Sunday newspaper coupon inserts can save you hundreds of dollars yearly. They are on line in your e-mails or at the product manufacturer's website.

There are websites that list the upcoming coupons in Sunday newspaper inserts. This is an important organizing tool because you can file the insert according to the publisher and the date it was delivered in the newspaper. Once it is filed you can add the list of coupons to the front of the insert and know at a glance what is actually in the insert without having to go through it to get the coupons that you need for that week's shopping trip. This list serves as an index to the coupons in the newspaper coupon inserts.

In my area, there are several coupon inserts included on most weekend newspapers. They are Procter and Gamble, Red Plum and Savers Source.

I ask other people who are not going to use theirs, to save them for me. This way I have several copies of the coupon inserts. If a really good deal is available for any of the coupons, having several copies of the insert enables me to stock up on items at lower prices. I take the coupon inserts out of the weekend paper and file them with the list of coupons that are included in that insert. Websites such as http://www.sundaycouponpreview.com will even e-mail the lists to you. You can print them out and add it to the files of inserts. This will give you an instant inventory of coupons that you can use.

The best way to use your coupons is to check them against local sales. I always try to use a sale price, a manufacturer's coupon and a store coupon together to get the best deal that I can. I follow websites such as: http://www.tipresource.com, because they have done the tedious task of putting together the "deals" that will work at major chain stores that may be in the area. This way everything comes together the sale price, the store coupon, the manufacturer's coupon or other options, resulting in the best price.

One other website that I follow is: https://savingstar.com. This site enables you to make money on the items that you purchase (in addition to sales and coupons). There are certain products that they list and you add to your account. When you purchase these products, they will add a certain amount of money to your account. When your accumulated funds hit $5.00, you can request a payout.

There are products that have muliple deals available. If you complete all of these deals, you can actually make money.

Here is an example of a recent deal.

Wisk detergent was on sale at a local pharmacy for $2.99 (usually $3.99).

**$2.99 x 2 = $5.98**

I had a pharmacy quarterly coupon booklet coupon for $1.00 off two bottles.          **$2.99 x 2 = $5.98**
              **-$1.00**

I had two manufacturer's coupons for $1.00 off of one bottle.

**$2.99 x 2 = $5.98**
         **-$1.00**
         **-$2.00**

This makes the price of both bottles $2.98, only $1.49 per bottle.

I did this deal until I had spent a total of $15.00 on Wisk detergent. After my purchase was recorded by Saving Star I received another bonus of $3.00 for purchasing the detergent. That meant that after totaling up all the accumulated deals on this product, I received 5 bottles of detergent and paid less than $4.50 total for them. That's less than $1/bottle.

In my opinion, it is worth it to take the extra time and use coupons to get the products that I cannot easily make on my own. I use this method for things that are necessary such as printer ink, personal hygiene products, and clothing or for things that are indulgences such as ice cream or candy. I love to use it to back up the canned goods that I grow in my garden too.

**Make It**

There are times that even using sales, coupons and rebates for an item still leaves the cost more expensive than you want to pay. In that case, if you can make it, then you should. A good example of this is making your own laundry soap. Many times it is cheaper, better and healthier for you if you can make your own cleaners. There are many sites on line to give you recipes and instructions on making your own soaps. You might like to start with Mother Earth magazine and website for some of the best recipes.

Making it yourself doesn't only apply to detergent and other soaps. Use your imagination! You could make your own clothes, or do your own house repairs, or lawn maintenance. You can make yourself capable by learning how to make simple and eventually more sophisticated needs around your home.

When you learn how to do something, it makes you more valuable to others around you who might need your expertise and knowledge. Who knows, someday you may want to barter your knowledge and effort for theirs. It is especially important to have unique skills during an emergency.

### Second Hand

When you are looking for an item that you can't make or find for free; look for second hand items.

There are many second-time-around shops in cities and towns across the country. Many of these shops have the added bonus of supporting people who are in need of jobs and training, or they support another type of charity. Goodwill Industries even has an online presence where you can find items for sale.

You can save on gasoline by calling shops first to find out if they have what you are looking for. It might be best to look for yourself though, because you could spot something that you weren't necessarily looking for at this time, but is a great buy.

Clothes, jewelry and kitchen necessities are commonly found in second hand shops. There are also some other great finds at greatly reduced prices waiting there too.

**Garden Produce**

If you have any space outdoors or inside, you can cut your grocery bill. I have always had a garden. If it did not produce all of my fresh vegetables, at least it would produce some of my table fare. A package of seeds is a small investment for the large amount of produce that will be yours.

Getting seeds can be free or cheap. Most people are happy to share, if you show an  interest in their garden. Listen carefully to what they have to say because they have planted in your area and they know what will work best for your local climate and soil type.

Make sure to take a trip to the library and read about gardening before you commit to a garden. There are many good books about gardening in every locality. There are also produce calculators that can be found on line to help you decide how big your garden should be. Decide how many people you want to feed and how much of each vegetable you want to harvest. Then decide how big your garden should be with a garden calculator.

Talk with agricultural university experts from the local Ag Extension Office. This is a free service and will help you immensely; especially if you are just beginning to garden.

Gardening can yield healthy produce for you to fill your pantry. Gardening also helps to make and keep you healthy in other ways too. The added exercise will keep you moving and strong. Actually being involved in the day-to-day nurturing of a plant and forming a relationship with it will positively affect your own self-worth. Through planting and caring for a plant or many plants you become more knowledgeable and valuable. Gardening is healthy in so many ways.

**How To Preserve It**

Drying food is simple to do and it takes only time and effort, once the sun-drying frame is made.

There are quite a few frame-making directions on the internet. In essence, it is quite simple to make your own drying equipment.

Make a four-sided frame of wood and stretch screen over it. Attach the screen with nails or staples.  Repeat until you have enough screens to dry your produce.

Once you have layered the fruit or vegetables on the wire screening, then cover the top frame with cheesecloth or screening. This will prevent flies and other insects from lighting on the fruit and vegetables while they are drying. Leave the drying racks in a sunny, breezy area and check them often. Do not leave out overnight or if there is a chance of rain.

When the produce is dry enough, layer it loosely in jars and store in a cool dark area of your home.

There are many, more elaborate ways to dehydrate your produce, but this is the simplest. Purchasing an electrical dehydrator is another good option. They are relatively cheap (especially if you buy one at a garage sale or a second hand store) and very

reliable at producing healthy cheap food for your pantry and table.

Canning foods is also a great help. This is how I prepare most of my foods to be shelf stable. I love to grow and then prepare and can my own foods. I

have the personal knowledge that they are healthy, local and organic!

There are two methods of canning. The first is water bath canning and the second is pressure canning. Everyone should be taught how to can involving both methods. Some prefer to use one method more than the other but both have their uses.

Please get in touch with your local agricultural extension office and take a class on how to can foods properly. The subject is very involved and it is useful to have someone teach you. Knowing that you must follow the rules and guidelines is the most important information that you need to can your own foods safely. There are plenty of local organizations that will gladly teach you how to preserve produce. Check with churches, agricultural extension offices, co-operatives, health food stores and libraries. Most of these classes are free and open to the public. Definitely enroll and learn this health, wealth and life preserving technique to preserving foods.

**Overflow Produce**

Having a garden may create your own overflow of produce. You can preserve it for your larder and then use it yourself or you may consider trading it with others for their overflow. You could preserve it and then trade it. If you do this then make sure to value it higher than the non-preserved produce because of all the extra time and effort that has gone into your overflow produce.

I once was given free access to pick all the fruit that was still on the tree or ground in a friend's orchard. This included apples and pears. Another friend asked me to clean up their orchard that included some late blooming plums and some peaches. Added to a fantastic buy at a local grocery on grapes and we were able to make fruit cocktail which I canned. I definitely shared the "bounty" of canned fruit cocktail with both of the orchard owners. (Maybe it was a bribe in hopes of doing it again the following year!)

**Advertise**

There is at least one great "techie" way to get free food. That is to advertise for it. Put an ad on Craig's List and other free exchanges for any overabundance of produce that someone may want to share.

**Buy Seconds**

Most farmers "pick over" their crops and only sell what will sell best. The most beautiful and presentable fruits of their crops will likely sell first. If you ask for seconds or slightly bruised fruits and vegetables you will likely get a much better price. There is nothing wrong with this produce that will prevent it from being eaten. You may need to cut out a bruised or misshapen spot or have to use it very quickly, but it is worth the effort to have fresh produce at a reduced price.

## Buy in quantity

Buying in bulk from the big name stores makes sense sometimes, but so does buying produce in bulk. If you can make time to deal with the food properly, so that none of it will go to waste when you get it home, buying in bulk makes sense. Usually the more you buy the better deal you can get from local farmers. I once bought three cases of musk melon. What we didn't eat right away we packed in plastic containers and poured 7-Up on and then froze it for later use. Yummy treat in the winter!

## Buy at the end of the season

Farmers who have not sold all of their produce would like to sell it all. That just makes sense. You would like to get a good deal on produce to fill your pantry. That just

makes sense. Asking to buy a farmer's end of season inventory at a reduced price will probably help you both.

**Buy from local farmers/gardeners**

Taking a trip to the local Farmer's Market will always be a delight! The sights and sounds always seem to make me hungry. Get to know the local farmers/gardeners. They can usually sell you what you are looking for cheaper than you can get it once it has travelled half way across the nation (or the world). There is less freight/travel cost involved.

The produce is fresher because of the shorter distances travelled and much of what you find at local Farmer's Markets is grown organically (although the farmer may not have gone through all the red tape involved in order to be labeled as "organic" when it is sold).

If the farmers don't have what you are looking for they will know where to point you so that you can find what you need. Making friends at the Farmer's Market can be very valuable.

**Gleaning**

As you drive to work or school, look at the yards with fruit trees in them. Most of the owners would rather not have to pick up the fruit when it is time to mow the grass. Ask them if you could pick it up for them and use it yourself.

Mechanical harvest has greatly reduced the work that farmers have to do and made their farms much more profitable. But many combines and harvesters leave grain, fruits and vegetables in the field. Ask permission to glean the leftovers after the harvest. You will be surprised at how much useable food was ignored by the mechanical harvesting of a field.

Planting a tree in the yard to provide shade and fruit is another way to get the most out of a purchase or gift. Then you will have a place that is cool and green and shady where you can rest in the summer and it will produce fruit for you to stock pile for the winter.

**Wild Plants**

*Marsh Marigold – a springtime edible*

There are so many plants to choose from in the garden, but that number is dwarfed by all the wild plants that are available for free! You don't even have to nurture them in a garden setting. All you have to do is to identify them and prepare them. They are everywhere.

Wild plants were used by early people for food, medicine and technology. We can still tap into this easily available source of nutrition and health today. To prepare yourself for the proper use of wild plants you should obtain (maybe at the library for free) a field guide to wild plants in your area. Familiarize yourself with the ones that are available at your local library. Remember though that not all plant guides were created equal. Only use ones that have the Latin nomenclature! Many times authors use common names for plants that they are familiar with. This leads to confusion when plants are discussed and compared to other plants that have the same or similar common names. Several that I can recommend as excellent field identification follow:

The Forager's Harvest, A Guide to Identifying, Harvesting and Preparing Edible Wild Plants
By Samuel Thayer

Forager's Harvest Press, Birchwood, WI

Edible Wild Plants of Eastern North America
By Merritt Lyndon Fernald and Alfred Charles
Kinsey
Courier Dover Publications

The Uses of Wild Plants, Using and growing the
wild plants of the United States and Canada
By Frank Tozer
Green Man Publishing, Santa Cruz

There is also
information that
can be used for
"herbals" or
medicinal
information. These
include:

The Earthwise Herbal, A Complete Guide to New
World Medicinal Plants
By Matthew Wood
North Atlantic Books, Berkeley, California

http://www.bio.brandeis.edu/fieldbio/medicinal_p
lants/pages/home.html

A good website to check out is the United States Department of Agriculture, Natural Resources Conservation Service. 2006. *The PLANTS Database.* http://plants.usda.gov. 18 November 2006. National Plant Data Center, Baton Rouge, LA 70874-4490 USA.

There are also several apps for smart phones that are available and easy to use in the field when you need to make a decision about a plant. Steve Brill has an excellent one available.

What is available?

Every part of the countryside has different plants that vary not only by region, climate and soil type, but by season also. It is imperative that you learn from as many reliable sources as you can. The best knowledge comes from people who know and use the local plants themselves. Look for local classes on plant identification and usage through the local agricultural extension office, State Master Naturalists classes, local university and college botany/plant classes, Herb Societies, Botanical Gardens, Farmers' or Agricultural Co-operatives, local tribal organizations, as well as local Organic Food Co-operatives. You may be surprised at the number of organizations and people who are willing to share their plant knowledge with you.

Most people have at least a basic knowledge of a few common plants. In a time of need, even that little knowledge will be put to use. It will really put you ahead of others, who are looking for the same resource plants as you, to know what plants are edible and which are poisonous.

Common Plants include:

**Dandelions, Taraxacum officinale**

Dandelions were brought to America as a food plant, and were originally grown in gardens on the

eastern seaboard. Today it is difficult to think of a landscape without the common dandelion. It is a good source for several foods. The leaves, when young and tender can make a delicious salad. When they are a little older, they become just a bit bitter, so they will need to be blanched or boiled for a short period of time and then the water that they were boiled in should be discarded. This should take care of any bitterness in your vegetable.

The dandelion root can make a decent coffee substitute. Pull the taproot by closing your hand around the main stem very close to the earth and slowly pulling. This should be done after a rain or when you have watered the area thoroughly so that the root will come out more easily. The root can also be dug with a shovel.

Once you have the root extricated from the ground, clean it by brushing with a vegetable brush and rinsing thoroughly. If the root is more than an

inch in diameter, slice it lengthwise before you place it on a cookie sheet. If it is a small root, it should not need to be sliced before drying. When a baking sheet is covered no more than one layer deep with the root, you can put it in the oven on the lowest setting (200 F) and slowly dry the roots. Check them after one hour to make sure that they are not overdone. Turn them as needed until they are thoroughly dry. After allowing the roots to dry put them in airtight container for storage. To make dandelion coffee simply grate or grind the dried roots and pour hot water over/through them. I use about the same amount of dandelion roots as I would coffee grounds, adjusting as your taste buds require.

Dandelion blooms can be dipped in a light batter and fried.

The leaves can be cleaned, dried and pulverized, then used as flour in many recipes.

### Goose Foot, Chenopodium fremontii

Another easily recognizable plant is lambs quarter, goose foot or gray leaf. The leaves of the lambs quarter can be eaten through the course of the summer because they do not get bitter like the leaves of so many other plants. Simply gather the leaves, rinse them clean and add a minimal amount of water to boil them in. When they turn to a bright green and are soft they are ready to eat. I serve the greens with a tiny amount of butter and salt to taste.

Later in the season when the seeds form on the lamb's quarter these can be harvested, ground and used for flour.

I am sure that there are similar regional favorites as the ones that have been mentioned. Please find a person who is familiar with plants in your area and go on walks with them. It is worth paying someone to learn their information on plants. (It is up to you, how you want to pay them! Time, Effort, Energy, Knowledge)

**Trees**

Most people have at least a few trees that they are familiar with and can name. Some of these include fruit and nut trees, which can provide wholesome foods that store easily.

If you are able to influence the choice of trees when they are planted or you are in charge of planting trees think about the many benefits that they can provide. The US Forest Service supports planting trees in strategic positions to shade walls and windows or provide wind protection for less power consumption for heating and cooling a home. There are also the fruits and nuts as well as possible energy production or other wood products that trees are capable of producing.

Trees can provide for so many of our needs that their placement and species choice should be carefully considered. Definitely make trees a part of your long term emergency preparations. There are government programs that can help to provide cheap trees. Information on these is available through your county agricultural extension office. Remember to ask neighbors when they are cleaning gutters for any "baby trees" that they find growing there or any other unwanted place, for that matter. Many times there are maple trees growing in flower beds or other places they don't belong, so don't be shy to ask for these seedlings. Maple trees fill my family's need for sweets through syrup and sugar. Getting someone else's unwanted trees helps them and you. You can then use their cast-offs to make a better prepared future!

### Meats

At a minimum, you
must make sure that
the meats you store in
your pantry are
healthy.  Visually
inspect meat that you
want to use. It should
be a "healthy" color,
depending on the meat
this can be a pink,
white, bluish (some

chicken), gray (some pork) or a red color. It should
NOT be green or black. Use your nose to make sure
that there is no tainted odor from the meat. Many
microbes let us know of their presence by odor. Put
that telltale clue to use for you. If it does not smell
like it should be eaten, then DO NOT EAT IT! When
you are inspecting possible meat sources take
notice of how the meat feels or its texture. It
should NOT be tacky or slimy. If you are buying
meat from a grocery store check the "use by" date
on the package and don't buy it after the use by
date. The use by date is the last possible date to
cook and eat the meat that you purchase as a fresh
meat. That means that you could purchase the
fresh meat with a short "use by" date and then

take it home and either can it or freeze it or dehydrate it (immediately) and it will be stable and edible past the "use by" date. In effect you have given it a new shelf life because the "use by" date would be pushed further into the future because you change the meat to have a longer life by changing the state that it is in. You changed it from a "raw" state to either a frozen, dehydrated or canned state.

Freeze, Can or dehydrate to save your meats. Here, education and knowledge are king! Here it is about meat storage. The best meat storage may be different for different emergency situations. Think about your individual situation and make decisions now on how to best prepare for your possible events. If the best possible is not attainable, then do the next best thing, but do something! Freezing your meat is easy in this day and age. There are directions on how to safely freeze meat on the net and through your local agricultural extension office for free. At 0 degrees Fahrenheit and below, microbes such as mold, bacteria and yeast are inactive (not killed). So, you must keep your freezer constantly below 0 degrees Fahrenheit to ensure healthy meat. Once the meat temperature goes above 0 degrees Fahrenheit, it should be thawed and thoroughly cooked before being eaten.

To thaw meats safely, place them in a refrigerator that stays below 40 degrees Fahrenheit for approximately one hour per five pounds of meat. Other safe thaw methods are available on line or through information at a county extension office for free.

Enzymes are not stopped when meat is frozen. The enzymes are slowed by freezing and this enables meat quality to last longer. Enzyme action on the meats 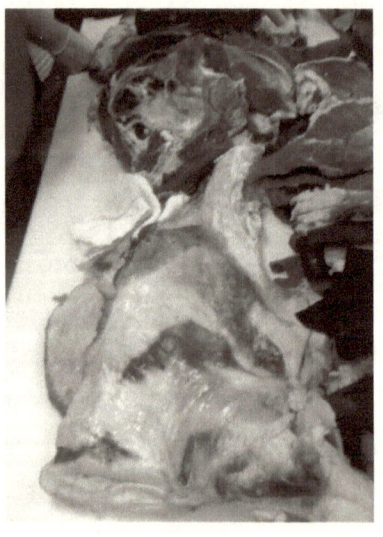 is not a health problem, but a food quality issue.

Wrapping meats in an airtight manner will eliminate freezer burn and keep meat quality high.

Here are a two good websites to check out about freezing meats.

http://www.four-h.purdue.edu/foods/Freezing%20meat%20and%20poultry.htm

http://www.wikihow.com/Freeze-Meat

Canning meats is an easy way to make sure that your meat is shelf stable and ready to eat. Following the canning directions that are available through the United States Department of Agriculture.

Drying meat is easy to do and can be available to do even during a disaster. The meat should be sliced very thinly and placed on a drying rack. The drying rack that you make can be made of sticks that are woven together to create a very open support for the meat. The rack should be placed near, but NOT OVER the fire. The fire should be close enough and in a good position to allow any smoke and heat to flow over the meat and keep any insects from touching the meat.

A more elaborate way to smoke meat is to build a "container" or "tunnel" to funnel the smoke to the meat.

In my area there are hickory trees and they provide a distinct taste when the wood is used to flavor the dried meat. If available, use new growth from the springtime. (These new growth twigs can be harvested in the springtime. They can be dried and then used to flavor the meat.)

There are several good ways to get free or cheap meat.

Think about the places where most people get their meat. Most people get their meat at the grocery from the butcher's section. Get to know your local butcher. There are plenty of small towns and large cities with small butcher shops. I know many of the butchers by their first name in my town and I frequent their shops. At first I paid full price and enjoyed the meat. Now I know what to ask for and I get wonderful tasting meat at less than what most people pay. You can look for cheaper cuts or know when certain meats go on sale.

I ask for liver and gizzards that can be ground and either added to other ground meats or eaten by themselves. They are very cheap and bring down the overall price of the ground meats. They also are very tasty.

I also ask for any fat that I can render and make into lard for cooking purposes.

An important part of working with many butchers is to not turn down any offer or deal for meats that you think are remotely useable. You do not want to offend a butcher!

**Your Own Overflow**

Another important source to remember is your own overflow (not just the butcher's). When I prepare meat for canning or freezing, I remove most of the skin (on chicken) and fat (from most meats). This saves room in my freezer or saves jars or shelf space.

But you don't want to waste anything that you already have in your possession. It is always cheaper to use what you have than to have to purchase or make it again. In order to use the fat that you trim from meat that you are storing or eating, cut it off and place it in an airtight plastic bag in the freezer. I keep a zipper-type closing bag in the freezer for chicken fat and one for pork fat and one for beef. I keep them separate because they have different properties that can be used in different ways.

Chicken fat can be frozen until you have enough to work with and then cut into small pieces. These small pieces can be used to make a simple lard for cooking. Pork fat that is trimmed from other cuts can be frozen and stored for use as lard. Rendering lard simply means heating the fat in a large, heavy container until the fat melts and boils. Any meat scraps that are included in the boiling process can be eaten. Traditionally these are called "cracklins" and are considered a delicacy in our area. Pour off the melted fat into a freezable container that won't melt (I use a metal container to catch and cool the liquid lard. Then I put it into a freezer container.) This white lard is tasty! Pork lard is a wonderful substitute for oil in most recipes. I love to make popcorn in lard! What a wonderful taste.

**Hunting**

Yet another way to get cheap food is to hunt for it yourself. Don't spend tons of cash on hunting.

Think like Early People. Native people in your area lived off the land. They may have traded for some things, but in most cases they used the resources around them and lived off the land in the local area. You can work with the land and it can help to keep you to be healthy and well fed.

Early people spent as little time on the actual hunt as was necessary. Today many people consider hunting to be a recreation and spend more time and money than is actually necessary to hunt. The method and time you allow for hunting can be seen as recreational and as preparing for an emergency.

Some of the early hunting methods include:

Snares

Slings

Spear/Atlatal

Dead Falls


Please check that you are within the law when you hunt for food. In an EOTWAWKI scenario, there may not be laws and rules to contend with, but there are laws now. Now is the time to learn to hunt and to practice until you are good at it, while still staying legal.

**Road Kill**

Many counties across the nation have a problem with deer that are killed by vehicles on highways and byways. In many of those counties, there is not an official way to deal with the dead deer. In other counties, officers must record and report the car/deer wrecks, but they do not have a way to get the deer off the road. Call your local law department (on the NON-emergency number) and ask if there is a list that your name can be added to for road kill alerts. This will ensure that you will be called when a deer or other large animal is hit and killed by a vehicle. You can use the meat to fill your freezer.

Once your name is on the list, make it easy on the law officers. Follow their directions. In my county that means go to the accident site as soon as possible and be prepared to take the deer immediately. Do not expect the law officer to help you load the deer. Always ask if you can or are allowed to field dress the deer at the accident site. Once you get home be prepared to butcher and prepare your meat for storage immediately.

There are alot of benefits from using roadkill deer for your larder.

1. You did not put any time into hunting
2. You did not have any cost into the hunting (no bullets or other, more expensive equipment)

3. Most meat is very healthy. (Check out the cost of "Free Range" meat at the supermarket - because it eats what it wants when it wants to and so did your deer)
4. Delicious meats that are not the ordinary fare for many people

Disadvantages of road kill meat

1. You have to respond immediately to the call for road kill. This can be inconvenient sometimes. I have found that most deer in our area get hit in inclement weather and after dark. It makes sense to have a "ready bag" just for when you get the call that there is a roadkill waiting for you. If you have everything in one place, you won't forget a vital piece of equipment to make

your life easier. If you put all of your field dressing equipment together, it is easier and quicker to get to the roadkill site and be able to field dress it at the site as well as put it into your vehicle quickly and safely.

2.  It may not be what you expected.

a.      I have picked up carcasses, that, once I got them home, and looked them over, I didn't think that it was worth the effort to butcher it. I always inspect it for health of the meat first and for ease of butchering. Only butcher what you think is healthy meat! If too much time has passed since the animal died, do not even take it home. Tell the police officer or Department of Natural Resources officer that you have to pass on this animal for whatever reason.

b.      If the animal was hit in such a way that the meat will not be edible, or it will take too much time to butcher it, then do not waste your time by bringing it home. Remember that all costs are related to either: Work, Time, Knowledge or Money. Your time and work are valuable, so do not waste them on something that may not be what you want to eat.

Another way to bring home food is by fishing. Having your own pond would be optimal, but using state and federal property and following all the rules and laws allows you to hunt or fish and not own a property that is expensive to purchase and maintain.

## CHAPTER 11: CLOSING

This book teaches a way to see purchases as more than a price tag on an item. You should be able to think about the costs that went into an item as well as what an item can cost you. All purchases can be seen as an exchange of commodities, including Money, Time, Energy/Effort, and Knowledge. Money is not the only way to get what you need. If you are willing to spend extra Time, Effort/Energy and your Knowledge you will be able to spend less Money!

By being vigilant and aware of opportunities that present themselves, you will be able to increase your preparedness for much less money than those around you who have not read this material. Be aware of your surroundings and the opportunities that will come your way, now that you have a few more ways to understand your environment, you will find it easier to look at many situations and find a way to make it work for you and your future. Be thoughtful as you prepare. Make sure of what you are bargaining for and be certain that the other person understands the deal as well. If both parties are happy with the end result – It's a good deal!

This book brings thoughts together to help you become prepared for the future in a very low cost monetary way. If you spend less money on what you can make, find or bargain for, then you will have more money to spend on the things that you can't use Time, Effort/Energy or Knowledge to obtain. Hopefully you learned a few things, or remembered a few things. Try to be in "Prep Mode" all the time so that you do not miss an opportunity to become more prepared. Keep a good healthy relationship with God and the rest will follow!